The Art of Long Reining

Sylvia Stanier with Princess Henri de la Tour D'Auvergne's Le Marquis and her own mare, Fanny (circa 1966).

The Art of Long Reining

Sylvia Stanier

J.A. Allen
London

British Library Cataloguing in Publication Data
A catalogue record for this book is available from
the British Library

ISBN 0.85131.574.7

The Art of Long Reining – Third edition

First published 1972
Reprinted 1974
Reprinted 1976
Reprinted 1978
Reprinted 1979
Reprinted 1982
Revised edition 1987
Reprinted 1991
Revised edition 1995
Reprinted 1998
Reprinted 2001
Reprinted 2003

Published in Great Britain in 1995 by
J.A. Allen
Clerkenwell House
Clerkenwell Green
London EC1R 0HT

J.A. Allen is an imprint of Robert Hale Limited

Typeset in Hong Kong by Setrite Typesetters Ltd.
Printed in Hong Kong by Midas Printing International Ltd.

Illustrations by Maggie Raynor
Designed by Nancy Lawrence

To my distinguished friend and guide in the art of equitation
EINAR SCHMIT JENSEN
this book is dedicated

About the author

Sylvia Stanier began riding at an early age, and grew up with a hunting and showing background. Sam Marsh was one of her first teachers, and she has based much of her work on the principles of Lt.-Col. 'Joe' Dudgeon. Sylvia has travelled widely in both Europe and North and Central America. She has trained with Schmit Jensen and Oliveira, and attended the Olympic Games equestrian events in Japan in 1964, Mexico in 1968 and Munich in 1972.

In 1965, she won the Ladies Championship at the Dublin Show on Bachelor Gay. Riding Lough Thorn in 1966, she won the Lightweight Hunter Championship in Dublin, and later the same year, at Wembley, she gave a display of long reining with Le Marquis, during the Horse of the Year Show. In 1967 she won the Dressage Championship of Ireland, on Fanny.

For many years Miss Stanier worked at the Burton Hall Establishment. She has written a number of articles and books on training and riding, including the companion volume to this book, *The Art of Lungeing*, and now spends her time teaching and demonstrating in the UK and abroad.

C'est la légèreté qui donne à la fois à la haute équitation son veritable cachet, et à l'écuyer qui la practique le veritable caractère de son talent.

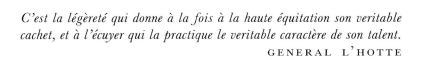

GENERAL L'HOTTE

It is lightness that gives haute école its true distinction and the rider who practises it his true talent.

Contents

List of Figures

List of Plates

Photographs by G.A. Duncan, John Evans, Fiona Forbes, John Stonex, Peter Sweet.

The author is working Pedro by kind permission of Mary Chipperfield.

Introduction

When I first wrote *The Art of Long Reining*, in 1972, I wrote primarily about the training method used by my teacher, Einar Schmit Jensen — that is, the Danish method. I felt that it was a good idea to put on paper his way of doing things because it had been of such immense help to me, and needed to be preserved for posterity.

Later, I found many people asking me if I could put something on paper appertaining to the English method of long reining. So, for the second edition of my book, I decided to add a section to try and cover in a more comprehensive manner this second way of using long reins. Now, for this third edition, I have added chapters addressing other matters I am asked about — how aspects of conformation influence the exercises we do on long reins, and what the progressive sequence of exercises should be. Also, to supplement the chapter on cavalletti, I have included an explanation of jumping on long reins.

When people talk about long reining it is usually as if there is something mysterious about it. So I hope that in producing this book I have been able to clarify what long reining is all about, and that it will tempt those who want to school and improve their horses into trying their hand at it.

The long reins are another medium through which schooling exercises can be performed. This book describes how to do them, commencing with the usual basic ones, and leading up to the greatly advanced collected exercises. Naturally, the idea is that it is then possible to ride the horse in these exercises, after having taught him on the long reins. Further to this, questions which people quite often ask are: 'What happens when I ride the horse?'; 'How does the horse adjust to the rider's aids?' In simple terms, long reining is usually started during the initial breaking-in period, being interspersed with other aspects of breaking. The horse may be learning to carry a rider for say half his lesson, and be working on long reins for the other half. Therefore, the systems are concurrent.

By the time the horse is ready to be schooled at an advanced level on long reins, he has already learned to carry a rider and obey simple aids. Thus, the idea of long reining is to teach the horse in as easy a way as possible the work and movements we want him to perform when he is ridden, and to improve movements or introduce new ones during further schooling.

All types of horses can be worked successfully on long reins and I feel sure that people particularly interested in the FEI driving competitions may find something to interest them, as well as pony, hack and riding horse owners — this book is not meant to be confined to any one sphere. Indeed, it has actually surprised me that I have worked so many different kinds of horse successfully through the long reins.

Schooling horses, for whatever purpose, can be fascinating and I for one find it never more so than on long reins, where there is the added pleasure of seeing as well as feeling the horse's reaction.

When people read this book I hope they will look carefully at the photographs. They are interesting because of the different breeds of horse which I have used. The frontispiece shows Le Marquis, a lovely little Thoroughbred, and I would particularly like readers to study his collected work, together with that of the Andalusian Pedro — two completely contrasting breeds, but still doing the same things and both in harmonious self-balance. Then there is Adel, the Oldenburger, also showing correct movement. All these are shown working in the Danish method. Hussein, the Arabian, is shown working in the English method; the horse is in a longer outline, suitable for a younger horse. Fanny, who also appears in the frontispiece, was Thoroughbred × Irish; she not only went on long reins but also hunted, evented and showjumped.

In rearranging this edition of *The Art of Long Reining* I have expanded into the realms of real schooling, that is, gymnastic schooling. Some of these exercises are quite difficult and should really be performed in a logical sequence, not in isolation, i.e. do not try the most advanced one first!

The idea of the schooling is to produce a well-balanced supple horse, which I hope I have illustrated in the very last photo in this book. Long reining is a medium through which the ridden horse can be produced, not an end in itself.

Chapter 1
Working the horse from the ground — first thoughts

The use of long reins as a method of training horses is not new. In fact it is really necessary to study the whole art of equitation to understand all the reasons for, and the objects of, their uses. Schooling horses from the ground was favoured by nearly all the great Masters and was included in the methods of the various European schools. The Neapolitan school of the sixteenth century used long reins and Antoine de Pluvinel used to school horses on long reins in the early seventeenth century.

Lungeing, work in hand, and work in the pillars are other ways of schooling horses from the ground.

When considering the objects of schooling an individual horse on long reins the job chosen for him should be taken into account — whether he is to be a hunter, hack, eventer and so on. This gives us an idea of our specific objectives. Of course, there are also universal aims which are to gain the horse's confidence, build supple muscles and give him a good mouth and manners. Whether in a young horse, or in re-schooling an older one, these objectives remain the same. Basic training in fact — but training need not stop at the basic stage, either under saddle or long reins.

All dressage movements, up to and including Grand Prix

work, can be achieved in long reins through logical and systematic schooling. The work can be done without the horse having to carry a heavy weight, you can see what you are doing, and there also develops a great mental rapport between handler and horse. Long reining is not an infallible method — any more than any other form of training — but it is capable of giving very good results.

When to start a horse on long reins and how long to stay with the method is a matter of personal preference. Once a youngster will carry a roller and lunge well, a course of three or four weeks on long reins can be very beneficial. For this work I would probably advocate the English method, working the horse each day throughout the course for approximately 20 minutes. For a dressage horse of Elementary Level or above I would most certainly use the Danish method, through which greater elevation of the forehand and greater collection can be attained more correctly. With such a horse, I would probably use the long reins once or twice a week (more if necessary) all through his competitive career, again for approximately 20 minutes at a time.

Chapter 2
Various methods

Different schools of equitation have, over the years, developed differing methods of using long reins. These differences, which are reflected in the equipment used, arise mainly from the varying purposes for which long reins are employed. As with other aspects of equitation, ideas which originated in one particular classical school have often been 'exported', as eminent trainers from certain countries have been influenced by the ideas of Masters from elsewhere. This 'cross-fertilisation' of ideas is a continuing process so, while the following descriptions of the main methods define them by their country of origin, that is not to say that they may not have their adherents elsewhere.

Danish method
This method, which appeared to be derived from the old Neapolitan style, was developed by a Danish colonel, Egede Lunde, and later used with great success by Einar Schmit Jensen.

The horse wears a driving pad or roller with terrets through which the reins run before being attached to the bit rings or cavesson headcollar. The reins run from the driver's hand direct to the driving pad. They do not normally go round the horse's hocks, but across his back. With this method a horse can be schooled to a very high degree with a very light

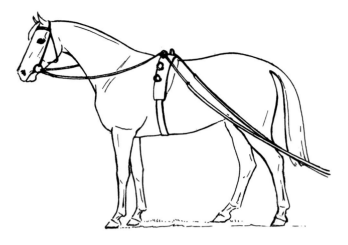

Danish method

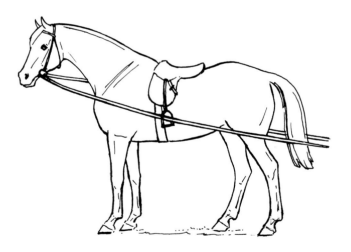

English method

Figure 1 Various methods of long reining.

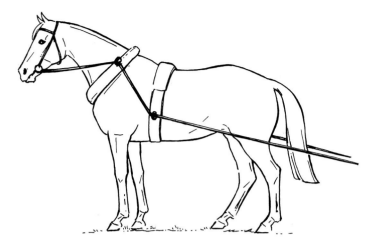

French method

Viennese method

contact, whilst carrying himself in a normal position, thus allowing the horse to develop the natural brilliance of his gaits.

English method

With this method the horse either wears a roller with rings on the sides, or, more likely, a saddle with the irons and leathers (which are tied to each other underneath the horse's stomach by a strap) used for the reins to run through. The reins then extend along the horse's sides, past his hocks and thence to the driver. This method can be used to mouth and gain control of a very young horse, but because of the very low position of the reins there is a tendency for a horse to overbend.

French method

In the French military school at Saumur, long reins are sometimes used in the basic schooling of young horses. Their method differs from others mentioned because, in addition to a roller, the horse wears a collar; the idea of which is to prevent the horse from lowering the neck too much or becoming overbent.

Viennese method

This method differs from the other three as it is used to show off a horse who is already very highly schooled under saddle, whereas the Danish method is usually used to school a horse up to a high degree, and the English method is used almost entirely on young horses. In Vienna, the Riding Masters walk close to the horse's quarters using a pair of long reins attached to the bridle but without a surcingle or terrets for the reins to go through.

Chapter 3
Equine anatomy

The ultimate aim of schooling is to produce a horse who can be ridden in gymnastic self-carriage. In order to do this, some knowledge of conformation and anatomy is essential. Normally, discussion of such matters takes place on a highly scientific basis but, in this chapter, I intend to take a slightly different view — to look at those aspects which a practical horseman must take into account when deciding which exercises will best remedy deficiences and bring about improvement. In this respect, it is also necessary to take account of other factors — the horse's background, breeding, temperament and age will all require consideration.

Regarding conformation, assessment should be made both of the horse as a whole and of certain key features. For the riding horse, the back — the whole topline from neck through to quarters — is crucially important, as are the limbs, which carry and propel horse and rider. The old saying 'No foot, no horse' is very apt, since the feet have the ultimate responsibility of carrying everything. Other key features — sometimes not given the attention they merit — include the ribcage and the head. The former exists primarily to protect the major organs and the latter to house brains, eyes, mouth and nostrils but their size and shape can, as we shall see, have considerable influence upon the horse's way of going.

The Art of Long Reining

To begin with the back: the vertebral column, which runs from the head to the tip of the tail, contains along its length the spinal nerves. If the vertebrae which protect these nerves are damaged, the consequences will be very serious. Fortunately, in the area where the rider sits, the horse has large lumbar muscles. Properly developed, these both strengthen and protect the horse's back, and one aim of long reining is to assist such development before the horse is asked to carry a rider.

In general terms, a long-backed horse will have relatively weak lumbar muscles, while those of a short-backed horse will be strong, but stiff. Both have their problems. It will take time (perhaps a year or more) to develop and strengthen the muscles of a long back and a similar time to supple those of a short back. (Further to this; patience is often in short supply these days — 'instant horses' being preferred. However, animals are *not* machines. Despite advances in veterinary science, nutrition and breeding programmes, equine conformation and temperament are *not* always perfect and it is inevitable that horses will sometimes progress less quickly than their owners might wish.)

Another very important aspect of conformation, viewed with reference to the back, is the comparative height of a horse's croup and withers. An equality of height is best. If a horse is higher at the croup than the withers, he will tend to go on the forehand and be difficult to balance. It should be noted, however, that up to about four years of age, horses grow 'in fits and starts'. Therefore a youngster may appear, temporarily, to be higher at the croup than the withers (or vice versa), but this does not necessarily indicate his final conformation when mature. A good visual guide is to take a horizontal line from the middle of the shoulder blade to the· hip joint (*not* the point of hip); a more or less straight line should indicate a well balanced horse.

After the back, I would look at the horse's hips and chest, to see whether they were wide or narrow. A broad, deep chest ('good heart room') may be indicative of stamina but a

Figure 2 The upper horse is 'croup-high' and may tend to be on the forehand; the lower horse is likely to be better balanced.

very broad chest can be a hindrance, not only to the performance of lateral work, but also to the full use of the horse's shoulders. A narrow-fronted horse may have less strength and stamina, but should have the capacity to cross his legs well in lateral work. Similar criteria apply to the rear; wide hips indicate strength and (coupled with good hind limbs) the potential for the horse to carry his weight further to the rear, as necessary for self-carriage and collected work. However, a very wide-hipped horse may find lateral work difficult and may become ungainly when asked for lengthened strides. Again, a narrow-hipped horse may not be so strong, but

9

should find lateral work relatively easy. Finally, the horse should match, front to rear — it will prove very difficult for an animal who is wide in front and narrow behind (or vice versa) to move in a balanced, united fashion.

Regarding the head, a large, heavy one is not desirable in a riding horse, because the neck has to carry the head without difficulty. The head is a relatively heavy part of the horse's anatomy and, the easier it is to carry, the better balanced the horse will be. Additionally, the shape of the head — wide or narrow — can be of great significance. A horse with a long, narrow head will have a narrow jaw, possibly with sharp, narrow bars which may be oversensitive and give rise to bitting problems. Wider heads, with wider jaws, tend to avoid such problems. Furthermore, good width between large, kind eyes usually indicates honesty and good nature.

To summarise, visual assessment will give you a picture of the positive and negative points of the horse and thus assist you in planning your training programme. Training your eye to observe and assess conformation is, therefore, both fascinating and rewarding.

Chapter 4
Equipment

When schooling horses, it is essential that the handler wears appropriate clothing. In this respect proper riding clothes, developed to provide comfort and protection, are best. A hard hat (to current BSI standards), pliable, fairly roomy, gloves and either full length or jodhpur boots are essentials. When long reining (or lungeing) *do not* wear spurs — they may cause you to trip over your own feet. Footwear which offers no protection should be avoided, as should any outer garment that flaps or rustles, or restricts your movement.

In these insurance-governed days, it is advisable for anyone who schools horses by any means to take out a personal accident insurance policy.

Equipment for the horse
The first essential is a pair of long reins, about 7·2 m (24 ft) in length, made of some light but strong material (either plaited nylon or thin canvas is good) with the last 2·4 m (8 ft) nearest the bit to be of rolled leather. This will slide through the terrets of the pad or roller easily, and does not wear out. The reins must be single — not joined to each other. Good clips for easy attachment to either bit or cavesson ring are essential. (In the English method, a pair of rope plough lines

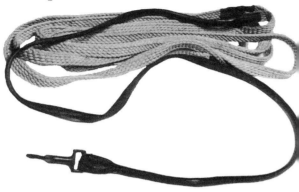

Plate 1 The long reins: (top) plaited nylon with leather front part — all of which is very pliable; (left) 'plough line' type rope, a strong line but not so pliable as the plaited nylon. This rope is shown neatly folded and tied, easy to carry or hang up.

Plate 2 Cavesson headcollar with rings attached near the horse's jaw, especially for long rein work. The front rings are usually reserved for lunge work.

can be used as long reins.)

A snaffle bridle or cavesson headcollar is best. It is possible to work a horse on long reins in any type of bit, but it is more usual to employ a mild snaffle, and this is certainly safer for the less experienced handler.

The driving pad or roller should be very well padded; it may assist if there is a pad underneath it. There should be three sets of terret rings on either side of the pad (six rings in all) — high, medium and low. Each set of rings is used for a different purpose — usually the highest set for the better-schooled horses, the medium set for young horses (whose head carriage is lower), and the lowest set for problem horses.

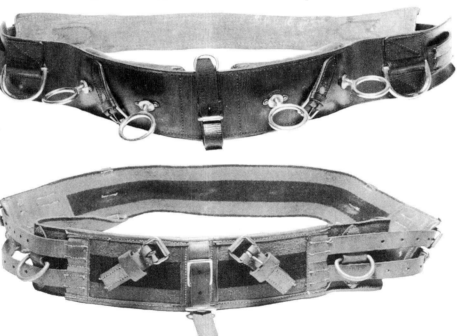

Plate 3 The driving pads: (top) leather roller with brass rings (terrets), suitable for the Danish method; (bottom) webbing roller with 'D' rings, suitable for the English method and for lungeing.

Both pads have adjustable girth buckles on either side, and attachments for bridle reins and crupper.

13

The Art of Long Reining

The roller used for the English method will only have the low rings — a saddle with stirrup irons (through which the reins can pass) tied to the girth is also acceptable.

There should also be some sort of attachment on the top of the roller for securing bridle reins if they cannot be detached from the bridle; and a crupper attachment is useful to ensure security. For convenience, position the roller so that it can be unbuckled from both sides of the horse.

A long whip will be necessary; a lightweight fibreglass one is probably the most suitable.

Especially for more advanced work — lateral movements, exercises with cavalletti and jumping, many people like to fit protective boots.

Plate 4 The crupper. A nicely padded lightweight leather crupper.

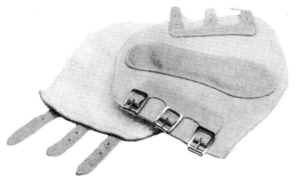

Plate 5 A pair of leather protective boots lined with sheepskin.

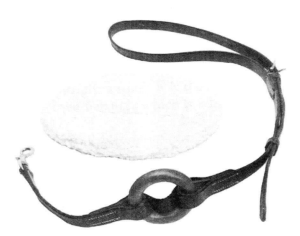

Plate 6 A leather side rein with a strong rubber insert. A nice small woollen wither pad.

Regarding side reins; these, used with discretion, can help put the horse in a correct outline by working him up to a contact through the engagement of his hind legs. They should, however, be introduced gradually − fitted loosely at first − and should *never* be used to pull a horse's head in. The use of side reins is discussed in more detail in *The Art of Lungeing*.

15

Plate 7 Tack fitted correctly to the horse's head — note that the rope rein has been attached to the ring situated behind the bit ring. The bridle is underneath the cavesson but the cavesson's noseband is inside the bridle. (Hussein.)

Chapter 5
Starting off

This is probably the most important stage, because if the horse is not started off correctly he may never become properly used to the reins. Any horse who is to be schooled on long reins ought to have at least some idea of how to go on the lunge. Long reining is the next step after lungeing in the education of a young horse. The aids are: the reins; the whip (which is, of course, used with great discretion); the position of the trainer (in relation to the horse's position); and the voice.

A word first on *where* to work. The best place is either an enclosed outdoor manège or indoor school. For one thing if a horse gets loose he cannot go too far, and the walls of the school are useful later on when doing certain lateral movements. If you *are* working in an open space (which is perfectly feasible with an experienced horse), have one rein ex-terret, as this can be used as a lunge line in event of emergency.

Fitting the tack
Having fitted the cavesson and the roller, the next step is to attach the lunge line, in the usual manner, to the cavesson. Then, standing on the left (nearside), with the lunge line still in the normal position, attach the second rein. This should go through the middle terret of the roller, on the right (offside) of the horse down to the cavesson, using the side ring.

Plate 8 Fixing the bridle reins: (top) the preparatory twist of the reins before placing them through the leather buckle on the pad; (bottom) the reins are now fixed through the buckle.

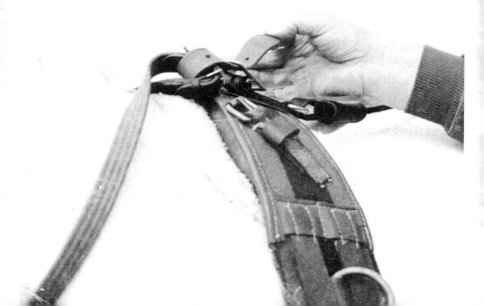

Once the equipment is fitted, allow the horse to walk round quietly on a circle, just getting him used to the second rein. An assistant can be useful in these early stages, particularly when you comes to work on a circle to the right — usually the more difficult side. To do this, the tack is fitted as before, except that the right rein is the lunge line and the left rein the second rein. When using this method, *never* put both reins through the terrets until the horse is completely calm and used to the reins. This may take several days or over a week, according to the horse's temperament. Always work quietly, doing a little at a time.

Another way of commencing is to have an assistant who lunges the horse and has control, while the trainer works the long reins, which are then put straight through both terrets almost immediately. This method is very useful when you go

Plate 9 Working on a simple circle. (Hussein.)

to change direction for the first time, as it prevents the horse getting out of control should he not like the feel of the reins on his back. Note, however, that apprehension should be overcome by touching the horse all over with the reins at the halt, so that he becomes so used to them that it is no surprise to feel them at any time later on. Once this has been established, a big step has been taken towards being able to rein properly. I cannot stress enough how important all this preparation is. For example, a basic change of rein is actually achieved by making the horse perform an 'S' bend with the horse moving in front of the handler, who passes the reins over the horse's back; the handler then changes to the horse's other side by passing behind the horse. This movement should be performed on a large 'S' bend, with a gradual change of

Plate 10 Circle right, reins through both terrets. (Adel.)

direction. In the early stages, have an assistant walking at the horse's head if there is a danger of the horse becoming frightened. If the assistant has the horse on a lunge line, this should be fastened to the centre ring of a cavesson noseband, to facilitate the changes of direction.

Handling the reins

The position of the trainer plays a big part in the correct use of long reins. You must be sure to watch the horse's hind legs and work the reins in rhythm with them (although, in the first instance, it may in fact be easier to look at the forelegs because each hand and rein should be used only as the horse's corresponding foreleg is in the air; that is, the trainer's hand should take up the left rein as the horse's left forefoot is in the air, thus creating an even contact in rhythm with the horse's movement). The aim is a steady hand, which gives kind but definite requests with a light contact.

Rhythm is all important in this sort of work. The hands should take up any slack in the reins, but *never* pull backwards and never have a dead hold on the reins. The trainer should usually be slightly behind the horse's inside hip, so as to encourage forward movement (moving towards the shoulder slows the horse down). The outside rein gives the degree of balance, the inside rein gives the flexion.

Most of the time, you should carry the whip behind yourself, but occasionally it is convenient to put it across from the right hand and allow it to rest on the left forearm. The whip is used to encourage impulsion and, at certain times, to guide the horse.

The nearer you walk to the horse the more control you have, but to obtain the nice light feeling, which is of paramount importance, you should be about 3−4.5 m (10−15 ft) from the horse. Position and distance vary according to the exercises being undertaken, but it is important to be able to follow the horse's movements easily at all times.

21

Chapter 6
Early exercises — Danish and English methods

With these early exercises, both at walk and trot, the first thing to implant in the horse's mind is that he should relax. While he must always be going forwards, he should work the bit with a closed mouth, and show no signs of tension. This should also get the horse using all his muscles correctly, particularly those of the back and neck, thus creating a correct, rounded outline.

Once the horse has learned to walk and trot round calmly on both reins in the manner described, the time has come to think about putting both reins through their respective terrets. It is possible to execute a change of rein with only one rein through a terret, but I prefer to have both reins in their proper position as soon as it is safely possible. The question of when to attach the reins to the bit is purely a personal one; some people prefer to start working from the bit as soon as possible.

Aids, circles and changes of direction
The circle is the first basic exercise and, within it, transitions to walk and trot. Later on, the canter and its transitions can be practised. Large circles, at least 12 m (40 ft) in diameter, are best for young horses. The halt and standing still are also very important exercises for any young horse, and can be taught fairly easily on long reins. By using the voice quietly,

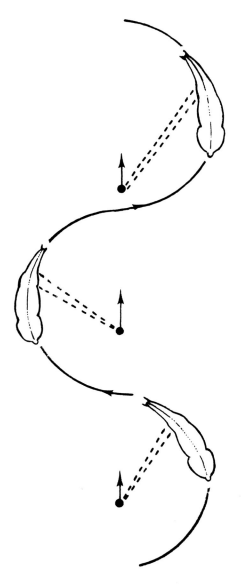

Figure 3 The serpentine — a series of changes of direction. The horse passes in front of the trainer.

positioning yourself more in line with the horse's shoulders and feeling the outside rein more strongly than the inside rein, you can usually obtain the halt. It may help in the first instance to do this several times in the same place; that is, utilising association of ideas, which can soon be transferred into aids proper. The horse should learn to stand quietly until asked to move. This, in itself, is a most useful discipline for any horse, and it will help to encourage the horse to look to the trainer (or rider) for instructions.

The aid to walk on will vary in degree from horse to horse, according to temperament. Sometimes an easing of the contact together with a quietly spoken 'walk on' will suffice, in other cases a light touch or sight of the whip may be necessary.

After these initial exercises comes the change of rein or the figure-of-eight. When changing direction you should work on the principle of giving with the outside rein as opposed to pulling with the inside one. This is important, too, when trying the serpentine; a series of changes of direction or loops (see Figure 3).

The value of driving the horse on straight lines should not be forgotten – this is one of the advantages long reining has over lungeing. When working the horse along the side of the school you can ask for a degree of self-carriage and lightness, while still encouraging free forward movement. Contact on the outside rein helps to keep the horse straight.

Chapter 7
The English method

The English method of long reining is where the reins come round the hocks. It is primarily for breaking-in a horse to the point where he can be ridden and controlled, whereas the Danish method is used where the intention is to go on to further heights of schooling.

In the previous chapter we looked at how to start a horse off on long reins, and various basic exercises. Much of this work pertains to both the Danish and English methods; the preliminary work is very much the same and, above all, the horse must know how to go on the lunge before you attempt long reining in any form.

Whether to use a saddle or roller for the English method is a matter of personal preference. Very often, with a young horse, it is a good idea to keep the saddle on, as it helps make him used to the feel of a saddle in all circumstances. However, the roller does a good job too and it is, of course, lighter. Side reins can be fitted to either saddle or roller.

Having accustomed the horse to the feel of long reins, which are usually attached to the cavesson (I prefer to use the rings underneath the noseband), proceed at walk with the outside rein through the 'D' ring of the roller, or the stirrup, and the inside rein direct to your hand. As mentioned previously, it is usually easier to start off on the left rein.

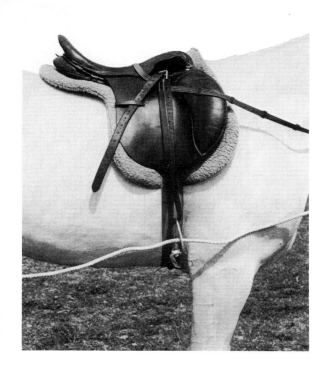

Plate 11 A nice saddle in position with stirrups tied and rein through offside (right) stirrup.

Plate 12 A strong webbing roller, with rein through the offside (right) 'D' ring. Note the stirrup (above) keeps the rein a lot lower down than the 'D' ring.

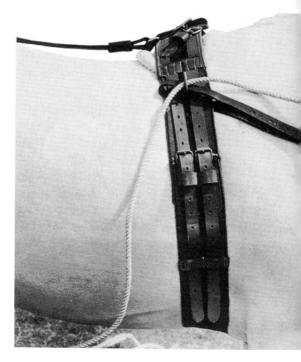

The English method

With the English method, the trainer's position will be different — much further behind the horse than with the Danish method. After the initial circles, much of the work will be on straight lines because one is dealing primarily with general control rather then performing specific dressage movements.

Whilst working on straight lines at walk, the halt can be taught, as can simple turns across the school. When halting, you can use the voice as well as the rein. You can even, if it is so desired, teach the rein-back — although this is somewhat frowned upon these days, the old trainers used to do it because they considered it taught the horse to respect the bit.

Plate 13 Horse fully tacked up, standing quietly ready to obey the handler. (Hussein.)

Plate 14 Horse now at attention and ready to move. Note how the reins are now in direct contact on a straight line back to the handler. (Hussein.)

Plate 15 Horse now in movement, going calmly. Note the inside (left) rein is not through the stirrup iron. (Hussein.)

Plate 16 *Horse working in side reins with a webbing roller and a crupper on.
(Hussein.)*

Plate 17 *Another view, showing the righthand side of the horse. The rope is
through the 'D' ring. Note that the side reins are comparatively slack in both
illustrations. (Hussein.)*

Plate 18 Just to show what can happen!

So, by using the English method, walking on, halting and turning from the walk can be taught and established. Trotting and cantering can also be taught on the circle but remember that you, the handler, must keep moving too, otherwise the horse may slow down when you don't want him to.

Lateral work *can* be taught with this method, but there is a danger that the horse can become overbent and, if you want him for dressage, he may learn the movements incorrectly. However, for control and teaching the horse his early lessons, it is an admirable way of achieving your goal.

Chapter 8
Advanced schooling — the Danish method

The question of advanced schooling always brings up all sorts of theories on equitation. How then does one proceed to the ultimate through the long reins? Obviously any horse being schooled in dressage will eventually be shown off under saddle, so the long rein work is used to help achieve a better result when the horse is ridden.

Collection and extension
When the horse does his early exercises well (that is, he learns to accept the bit in a relaxed manner, to change rein, to halt and to move on), then the time has come to begin improving his balance with proper engagement of the hind legs leading to collection and correct extension. Increasing and decreasing the size of the circles will help to teach collection and extension. The small circle which increases the engagement of the hind legs, and thus increases collection, should, however, never be smaller than will allow the hind feet to follow the imprint of the forefeet.

To achieve a proper degree of self-balance it is necessary to put the horse up to the bridle. This is achieved by positioning yourself further behind the horse, perhaps showing him the whip or touching him lightly with it round the hocks to encourage impulsion, which is then felt through the reins. As in riding, your fingers should work in rhythm with the

Plate 19 Collected trot. Note the horse is wearing a cavesson headcollar and no bit. (Le Marquis).

Plate 20 Extended trot. This photograph shows a horse in a maximum extension. (Le Marquis at the Horse of the Year Show, 1966).

horse's movement, keeping a contact with the reins, but never pulling backwards; thus the horse becomes light in hand.

To collect, one looks for a heightened yet energetic action, with a correct outline; the horse's head and neck are carried higher, with correct flexion at the poll and a relaxed jaw. All this is achieved by good impulsion and a rhythmic feeling on the reins. Extension, again, comes through good impulsion, and a slight easing of the reins, which allows the stride to lengthen.

The Half-halt
The half-halt is an extremely important action in long reining, creating as it does a new balance. The momentary increase in forward impulsion is taken up through the reins by the fingers, which then control and use that impulsion to rebalance the horse.

Canter
Canter, at first, is usually asked for out of trot on a circle. The aid is to produce an increased impulsion which is retained with the reins, the inside rein being felt rather definitely at the moment the inside hind leg is on the ground and the inside foreleg is off the ground. This can be reinforced by the voice command 'Canter'. To return to trot and, at a later stage, to walk, the outside rein is felt more strongly as the horse's outside hind leg steps beneath him, asking him to change gait in a balanced manner.

Once the trot to canter transition is established, walk to canter can be introduced, the aid being as follows. Having collected the horse, watch the hind legs carefully and, as the inside hind is *about* to come to the ground, keep an even contact on the outside rein and ask, with an increased flexion on the inside rein, for the strike-off. To begin with, after a few correct strides, return to walk and re-balance the horse.

When requesting canter from walk, or walk from canter, a good deal of concentration and precision are necessary, in order to apply the aid at exactly the right moment.

33

When cantering on a circle, remember that it should initially be big enough — at least 12 m (40 ft) diameter — to allow the horse to canter smoothly without loss of balance. As the horse becomes more supple, decreasing the size of the circle will increase the level of collection, but this must not be done beyond the horse's capabilities.

Gait variants

Walk, trot and canter can be practised in all their variations — collected, working (except walk), medium and extended, together with all transitions. The degree of collection or extension will be governed by the level of schooling at which the horse has arrived. Although, as previously stated, much of the work will be on circles of varying sizes, one of the advantages of long reins is the facility for working the horse on straight lines, and this should not be neglected when teaching the more advanced movements.

Rein-back

The rein-back is an important movement to teach any horse; it supples the back and causes the horse to become more obedient and better balanced. Care must, however, be taken in order that the horse does not become confused between the rein-back and the halt. The forward movements and halts from them should therefore be well confirmed in the horse's mind before rein-back is attempted, and the movement should be interspersed with halt to walk or trot, so that the horse learns only to rein-back on command, not by anticipation.

The aid to rein-back should be given by asking the horse to gain forward impulsion from a halt but, at the critical moment, instead of easing the contact and allowing the horse to move forward you should close the fingers on the reins in rhythm with the horse's shoulders and forelegs (that is, the right rein felt as the horse's right foreleg is raised), which will cause the horse to move backwards instead of forwards. This will eliminate any pulling back which, in any case, is entirely wrong since it will simply create hollowness and resistance. The aim, rather, is to have the horse moving backwards rhythmically in his own balance.

Lateral movements

These should be looked upon more as gymnastic exercises than as special movements in themselves. Their main purpose is to supple the muscles of the horse's back laterally and to obtain true flexion of all the joints. Correct lateral work therefore has a major part to play in making a horse equally supple on both sides — in other words, to alleviate the one-sidedness which naturally affects most horses. The circle is, of course, the first way of obtaining this type of lateral flexion of the whole horse — lateral flexions of the jaw are something different.

In teaching lateral movements along the wall, it is usually easiest to commence with the shoulder-out because, in this position, with the horse's head towards the wall, you can encourage him to move away sideways; once the horse understands this then it is a short step to the shoulder-in.

Plate 21 Shoulder-out along the side of the arena. (Adel.)

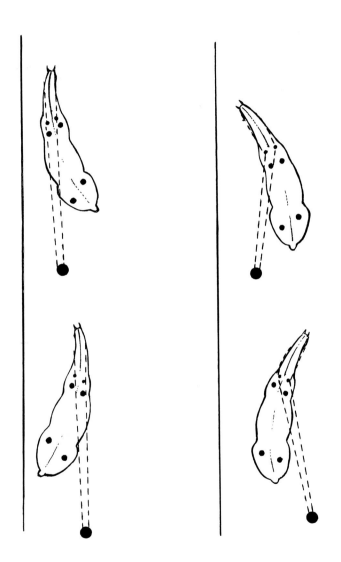

Figure 4 Travers and renvers.   *Figure 5 Shoulder-out and shoulder-in.*

Advanced schooling — the Danish method

Similarly, once the horse will move away from the handler in a lateral direction, the travers (Figure 4) should be relatively simple.

The shoulder-out or shoulder-in (Figure 5) can be performed on either three or four tracks; depending upon the degree of schooling and suppleness of the particular horse — but never ask for too much, too soon.

The easiest for the horse in the first place is a three-track movement, which can later be developed into the classical four-track movement if the horse is sufficiently supple. The most important thing to notice is that the horse is evenly curved throughout his length and that his neck is not pulled out to one side. The trainer, walking in a line just behind the horse's inside hind leg, should work the reins in rhythm with the horse's shoulders, feeling the outside rein as that leg is in the air, thus encouraging it to move sideways and forward, which will help the horse to keep in the proper position without losing impulsion. At the same time, the inside rein maintains the flexion.

In the shoulder-in (or shoulder-out) the horse looks away from the direction in which he is moving whereas in the travers and renvers along the wall (Figure 4), and in the half-pass across the arena, the horse should look towards the direction of movement.

You should, of course, start by teaching these exercises at walk, but later they can be performed at trot or, in some cases, at canter.

The turn on the forehand can also be performed on long reins. It is, essentially, shoulder-in on the circle which, when reduced to the minimum in walk becomes, in fact, turn on the forehand — the hind feet making a small circle while the forefeet mark time.

The same sort of thing happens with travers in walk on a circle — if reduced to the minimum it becomes pirouette at the walk — the hind feet marking time while the forefeet make the circle. This can be developed, in time, to pirouette at the canter.

Plate 22 Leg-yielding, horse moving to the right. (Pedro.)

Plate 23 Leg-yielding, horse moving to the left. (Pedro.)

39

When the horse can go readily from shoulder-in on a circle to half-pass, and vice versa, he is becoming truly supple. Further transitions from one lateral movement to another will dealt with in the next chapter.

Flying changes

If you master all the foregoing techniques, and are lucky enough to have a horse capable of more advanced work, then you will probably have formed a good idea of what is required for these advanced movements. The flying change (or change of leg in the air), can be taught through a simple change on the figure-of-eight, that is: collected canter-walk-canter on opposite lead. This of course, requires good timing in the use of the reins. With a great deal of patience this can be developed to produce changes of lead on a straight line, or the counter-

Plate 24 A flying change of leg at canter. Changing from the left lead to the right lead. (Adel.)

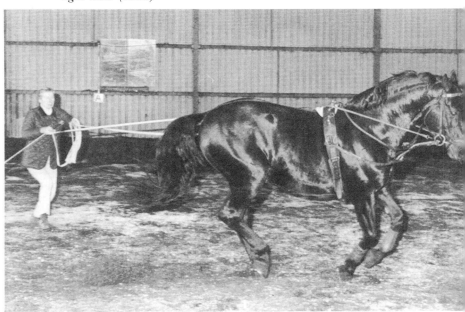

changes of hand at canter (a series of half-passes with flying changes of lead).

Piaffer and passage

I think that the long reins are a particularly good medium through which to teach or improve piaffer and passage, because the trainer can develop the self-balance, the lightness and cadence by watching the whole horse and using the finesse of the reins to bring out his brilliance.

Piaffer

Piaffer is the cadenced and highly collected trot in the same place, without gaining ground. Its development is character-ised by the lowering of the quarters, real flexion of all the joints, the correct rhythm of the steps and the elevation of

Plate 25 Piaffer performed by the Thoroughbred, Le Marquis.

Plate 26 Piaffer performed by the Andalusian, Pedro.

the forehand and forelegs. All these are easier for the horse to perform without the weight of the rider. Long reining gives the horse time to settle down and really learn this difficult movement without the rider's weight to distract him.

Passage
Passage is the movement in which the horse moves in a highly collected and cadenced trot containing a period of suspension. Development of the rhythm of passage is often obtained from piaffer, with the trainer just taking up the slack of the reins whilst maintaining the right amount of impulsion and balance. These are points which favour the use of long reins in the Danish style. So often horses show

uneven strides or other resistances such as setting their backs and mouths in passage, and these faults can be much improved without the weight factor of the rider.

Whether to teach passage before piaffer or vice versa is a matter of choice, or of a particular horse's needs. Some Masters prefer one way, some another. Decarpentry recommends trot to halt and then forward a few steps in passage. Baucher taught the *pas d'école* (school walk) first and based much of his high school work on that movement because it develops the suppleness of the horse's back, which is necessary for good performance of passage or piaffer. (The *pas d'école* and *pas de manège* are two movements belonging to the world of high school equitation. The former is a cadenced walk in two-time, in effect the passage at walk — true passage being the trot version of this movement. The latter is reserved for the horse ridden by the Commandant of the *Ecole de Cavalarie* at Saumur, in which the horse points his forelegs somewhat like a guardsman on parade.)

One thing is certain — the horse must not confuse the collected trot with the passage, so the aids must be kept clear. Depending, too, on the type of horse being schooled, you should decide on whether to ask for the '*doux*' or 'low' passage, or whether to ask for the spectacular high passage, really seen only in the high-actioned Spanish and Lippizaner horses.

According to the ability of the horse and the trainer, many other advanced movements can be taught to a horse through use of the long reins — the Spanish walk, the Spanish trot, the trot in reverse, the levade and other spectacular movements.

Chapter 9
Logical Progression

When talking about long reining, I often find that people are only looking for a quick method of breaking-in; or else that they are very much versed in their particular school of thought — English, French, Scandanavian, etc. The truth is that you may practice any of these methods of training so long as everything is logical. In general, adherence to correct principles and logical progression is of more importance than the detail of which 'school' is followed.

One should, therefore, have a programme and a set target. The programme can be built around the two criteria of straight line and lateral work, with collection and extension as further basic points. If we add to these the essentials of developing suppleness, instilling obedience and maintaining calmness, things should not go far wrong. Further to this, there is no doubt that, even though all horses are slightly different, correct development and suppling of the muscles will lead to easier performance of the next exercise. This is not wholly a physical matter; if correct muscular development makes it easier for a horse to perform a movement, he is more likely to remain calm and obedient whilst doing so.

The next point to consider is the immediate progression within a given movement; giving the horse a position, asking him through the aids and then allowing him to perform the movement requested — a classical and essentially simple formula which sometimes seems easier said than done.

Having, then, established these principles, we next have to consider the detail of what work to ask for, and in what sequence. I have set out below a sequence of exercises which, carried out correctly, should produce a well schooled horse.

Basic exercises
1) Walk the horse in straight lines.
2) Keep a feel on the outside rein and ask for a slight flexion to the inside on a 20 m circle.
3) Transitions halt to walk, walk to trot and vice versa.
4) Through corners with slight flexion to the inside.
5) Changes of rein with correct flexions at walk and then trot.
6) Shoulder-in position at walk.
7) Shoulder-out and shoulder-in.
8) Correct halt.
9) Rein-back.
10) Further upward and downward transitions, with accent on correct positions.
11) Collection and extension at trot.

Lateral work
12) Shoulder-in to travers and vice versa.
13) Shoulder-out to renvers and vice versa.
14) Shoulder-in to renvers and vice versa.
15) Shoulder-out to travers and vice versa.
16) Shoulder-in to shoulder-out and vice versa.
17) Travers to renvers and vice versa.
18) Small (15 m) circles incorporating various combinations of the above exercises.

NB. There are two schools of thought regarding the trainer's position when asking for travers or half-pass. (See Figure 7). If you use the English method, go to the inside and use the outside rein. If using the Danish method, go on the outside and ask the horse to walk away from you by means of a slight tap on the hindquarters.

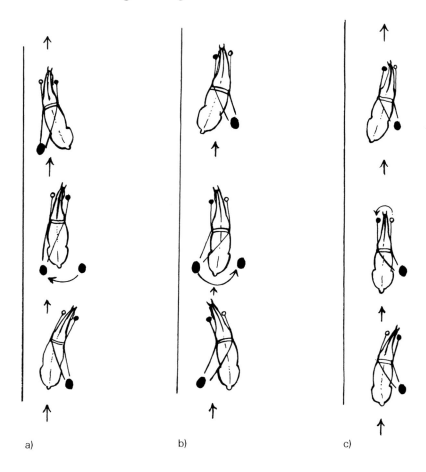

Figure 6 Aids for the lateral exercises.

a) Shoulder-in to travers (lateral aid to diagonal aid). Handler moves from right side to left side, passing the reins over the horse's back. Right rein is the active rein throughout.

b) Shoulder-out to renvers (lateral aid to diagonal aid). Handler moves from left side to right side, passing the reins over the horse's back. Left rein is the active rein throughout.

c) Shoulder-in to renvers (lateral aid to diagonal aid). Handler remains on right side — changes bend by easing from right active rein to left acting rein.

46

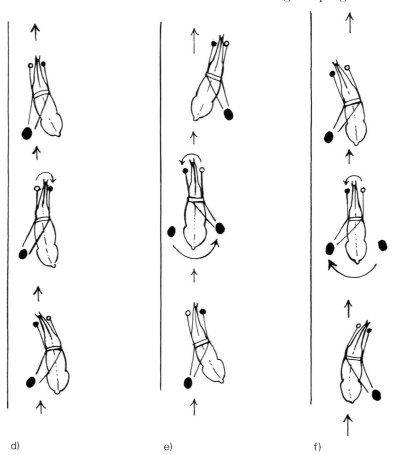

d)   e)   f)

d) Shoulder-out to travers (lateral aid to diagonal aid). Handler
   remains on left side − changes bend by easing from left acting
   rein to right acting rein.
e) Shoulder-in to shoulder-out (lateral aid to lateral aid).
   Handler moves from right side to left side, passing the reins
   over the horse's back. Changes bend by easing from right
   active rein to left active rein.
f) Travers to renvers (diagonal aid to diagonal aid). Handler
   moves from left side to right side, passing the reins over the
   horse's back. Changes bend by easing from right active rein to
   left active rein.

47

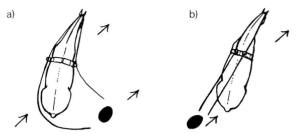

Figure 7 Two ways of moving the horse sideways.

a) With the reins around the hocks (as in the English method). The left rein helps to encourage the horse to move to the right. The handler is on the right (offside). The reins remain low and do not pass over the horse's back.

b) Here the reins are across the horse's back, so although the horse is moving right, the handler remains on the left side.

Both illustrations show horse moving to the right — to move to the left, reverse the aids.

Canter work

19) Correct strike off at canter on a circle. To begin with, this can be from a balanced trot, but should then be practised from walk.
20) Medium canter.
21) Collected canter.
22) Travers at canter.
23) Pirouette at canter.
24) Figure-of-eight at canter, with simple change of leg.
25) Figure-of-eight at canter with flying change.
26) Changes of lead every six strides, progressing gradually towards one-time changes (on a straight line).

Passage and piaffer

27) Work on increasing engagement and elevation of hind legs.
28) First steps of piaffer.
29) Consolidating piaffer.
30) Passage from either walk or trot.

Chapter 10
Work with cavalletti

Cavalletti are useful to improve balance and suppleness. They are particularly helpful in suppling and developing the muscles along the horse's back and neck. Horses can be worked on long reins over cavalletti very beneficially at either the walk or the gait best suited to working horses — the trot. It is easiest to work over a set of four cavalletti, and they can be used at all stages of training.

The spacing between cavalletti will vary according to the work of the day, the level of training of the horse, and his natural length of stride. When introducing cavalletti via walk, the spacing should be in the order of 0.8—0.9 m (2 ft 9—3 ft). For ordinary trot work, a distance of about 1.3 m (4 ft 6 in) is a fair starting point for most horses. In due course, collection and extension can both be practised. Spacing can be brought in to about 0.9 m (3 ft) for collected trot and brought out to 1.55 m (5 ft) or more for extended trot. However, it is important to start with the spacing easiest for the horse's natural working gait and to develop the more advanced work by degrees.

The height of cavalletti is usually about 10—15 cm (4—6 in) on their lowest setting and 23—30 cm (9—12 in) on their highest. I prefer to set them low to begin with, to avoid injury to the horse's legs (which can, of course, be booted or bandaged) or to the muscles of his back. Remember that muscles can very easily be damaged if worked beyond their capacity. It is the job of the trainer to develop, not destroy, muscles and, for that matter, to seek the horse's co-operation, rather than frightening him.

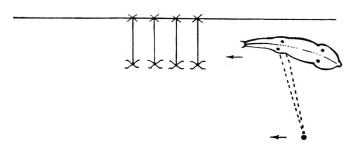

Figure 8 Cavalletti on a straight line to the left.

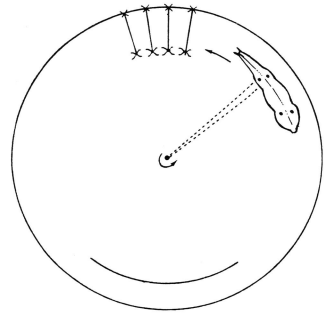

Figure 9 Cavalletti on a circle to the left.

The cavalletti can be placed either alongside the wall of the school (Figure 8) or, if the horse is unlikely to run out, on a straight line in the centre of a wide school. In the latter position, they can be approached readily on either rein from either direction. A further setting is to place them on a circle (Figure 9), taking care that the curve of the set of cavalletti corresponds to the curve of the circle. With this setting it is possible, as the horse progresses, to ask for slightly longer or shorter strides by moving the horse a little towards the outside or inside of the cavalletti, respectively.

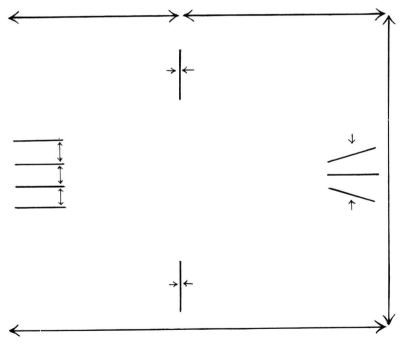

Figure 10 Various locations for cavalletti in a large school.

Chapter 11
Jumping

Jumping on long reins is a rather controversial subject but should, nonetheless, be described. The reasons for teaching and improving jumping on long reins are to develop the muscles and mental attitude and to improve handiness (steerability).

When jumping, horses use certain muscles in a slightly different way from when working on the flat. This is especially true of some muscles in the back and neck. The changes of balance required when jumping place different demands upon the horse from the movements of high school dressage — for example, the horse will have to make considerable use of the shoulders at the moment of take-off. This is not to say, of course, that the demands of jumping are entirely different from those of flatwork — indeed, a horse will have to be very supple and athletic to succeed in speed classes and will need to develop the full power of his hindquarters for the puissance.

Teaching a young horse to jump without a rider can be achieved by loose schooling or lungeing, and developed further by long reining. With the long reins you can:

a) Keep the horse straight
b) Control the stride
c) Change direction without stopping
d) Use a wide range of cavalletti, grids and constructions.

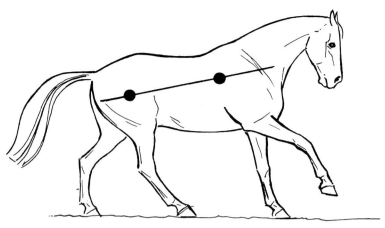

Figure 11 Balance for   *a) a dressage horse and*

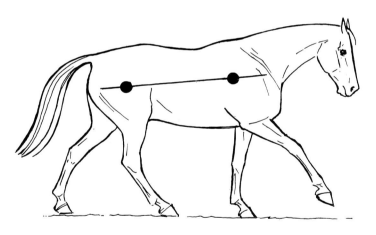

b) a jumping horse.

Just as in starting a youngster on the flat and training him through to all the high school movements, so you can lay the foundations of jumping and go on to a high level — although I would categorise piaffer and passsage as easier to achieve than jumping a seven foot wall! To reach such heights in

53

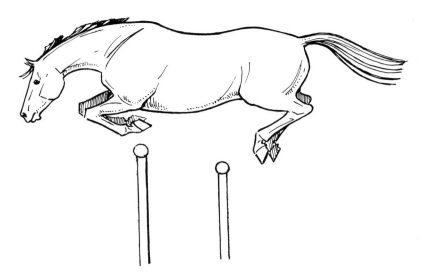

Figure 12 Jumping horse using his head and neck correctly, enabling him to pick up his forelegs properly.

both flatwork and jumping you do, of course, need a horse of great ability — which must be complemented by your own skill.

To return to basics, the introduction to jumping on long reins should be via walking and trotting over poles on the ground. Calm, rhythmical cantering and the development of a correct bascule then become top of the agenda. Shortening and lengthening the stride are also important — jumping horses need to be able to make these adjustments very quickly in competition. Further to this, long reining allows the development of the *horse's* eye for a fence. This is just as important as developing the rider's eye — indeed, there is an Italian saying: 'Master, you may shut your eyes, but mine *have* to be open.'

The fundamental criteria for jumping on long reins are that the handler moves quickly and 'gives' with hands and reins when the horse needs the freedom of his head and neck. In other words, as in all forms of jumping, the horse must not be jabbed in the mouth.

Regarding equipment, I would advocate a Danish-type driving pad, with extra-long reins. Do not use reins with loop ends – have them open ended so that you cannot get an arm or foot caught. If you do not wish to use a bridle, use a good, strong cavesson. I do not normally use side reins for jumping, as they are too restrictive.

Plate 27 The author on the Thoroughbred Lough Thorn showing a well-balanced happy horse; she never needed a bit! (Circa 1966.)

Conclusion

Working horses on long reins is a fascinating art. It rather depends upon the trainer's own particular requirements and theories as to which exercises are asked of the horse. However, from the mental rapport which one strikes up with a horse, one learns what willing creatures they are. From this alone, a great deal of pleasure can be derived, as it can from watching a beautiful horse give of his best in response to the slightest request.